AMPHIBIOUS TECHNIQUES

Modern Military Techniques

MODERN MILITARY TECHNIQUES
AMPHIBIOUS TECHNIQUES

James D. Ladd

Illustrations by
Peter Sarson & Tony Bryan

Lerner Publications Company • Minneapolis

This book is available in two editions:
Library binding by Lerner Publications Company
Soft cover by First Avenue Editions
241 First Avenue North
Minneapolis, Minnesota 55401

Library of Congress Cataloging in Publication Data

Ladd, James D.
    Amphibious techniques.

    (Modern military techniques)
    Previously published as: Combined ops. c1984.
    Includes index.
    Summary: Describes the various types of craft used
in a typical beach assault operation including escort
carriers, assault ships, helicopters, submarines and
tanks. Also discusses new technological developments in
amphibious warfare.
    1. Amphibious warfare—Juvenile literature.
[1. Amphibious warfare] I. Sarson, Peter, ill.
II. Bryan, Tony, ill. III. Title. IV. Series.
U261.L316 1985   359.9′6   84-10003
ISBN 0-8225-1379-X (lib. bdg.)
ISBN 0-8225-9505-2 (pbk.)

Manufactured in the United States of America

        5 6 7 8 9 10 93 92 91 90 89

CONTENTS

1 The Combined Operations Assault Force

An assault on an enemy beach is one of the most complex of all military operations. It requires careful planning, there are many decisions to be made before an amphibious assault force can be launched. One question is whether the landing should be by day or night. A night-time assault may cause the maximum surprise to the enemy. But with a large number of landing craft heading for a beach, there is less chance of accidental collisions in daylight.

Landings by several brigades would probably be made in daylight, but the landing of one brigade, as shown in the picture, would usually be made at night, provided the enemy's radar could be put out of action first.

The procedures are the same whether the assault is made by day or by night. The men who are going to make the first main assault, "the first

wave," are landed from helicopters or assault craft, which must be brought to the enemy coast in ships of the Assault Force. These ships include a type of small aircraft carrier known as a Landing Platform Helicopter (LPH) and purpose-built assault ships like HMS *Fearless* (11,600 tons) which can be seen in the picture. HMS *Fearless* carries four Landing Craft Utility (LCU) manned by Royal Marines, one of which can be seen near the ship. She also carries four smaller craft, LC Vehicle Personnel (LCVP), one of which is nearing the beach. A Commando Helicopter has flown from *Fearless* to land marines beyond the shore defenses.

The senior officers of the Assault Force plan the landing to come ashore where there are few, if any, strongly built beach defenses. The assault is then made in several stages:

1 Marines land before the main assault to knock out enemy radar, coast guns, and anti-ship missiles.

2 The first wave of marines land in LCVPs to capture enemy trenches behind the beach.

3 The second and third waves land to give the Assault Force a firm hold on the beachhead.

4 Tanks and artillery are ferried ashore by LCUs to build up the Force's strength on the beachhead.

5 The Force breaks out of the beachhead into undefended country behind it.

2 Command and Control

There are two senior officers commanding the assault: a Royal Navy Commodore in charge of the assault ships and a Brigadier in command of 3 Commando Brigade Royal Marines pictured here. Working closely with their staff, they plan the landing and arrange rehearsals on a friendly beach. Yet however carefully the landing is planned, they know that in any Combined Operation there will be some unexpected snag. They must be prepared to change their plans while the landings are taking place if the enemy have stronger defenses than expected, perhaps, or if the weather suddenly becomes rough and landing craft have difficulty in beaching.

To make such changes of plan, good radio communications are essential. These radio links, known as circuits and at one time called "nets," appear in the picture, showing how *Fearless* is a floating headquarters for the Commodore and the Brigadier. When the Brigadier's troops are ashore in numbers, he will take his headquarters to join them but keep in touch with the Commodore by radio.

Key to radio circuits—
from the LPD Fearless
1 To the Tactical HQ of the Commando unit with companies in the first wave. (Circuits to other Commando HQs not shown.)

2 To the flagship of the Admiral commanding the Fleet of which the Assault Force is part.

3 To the coxswains (coxs'ns) of LCUs (only one is shown).

4 To the Beach Master organizing the "flow" of men and stores across the beach.

5 To the helicopters flying from *Fearless* (only one is shown).

6 To the Ministry of Defense in London.

from the carrier, there are various radio circuits including: 7 to her helicopters, and 8 to her Harrier aircraft.

from the Naval Gunfire Support Officer

9 To an escort frigate to direct her guns at targets on the beachhead.

from the Forward Air Control Officer

10 To Harriers to direct rocket and bomb attacks against targets on the beachhead.

from each of the three Commando Unit HQs

11 To their companies' HQs (only one Commando's circuit is shown).

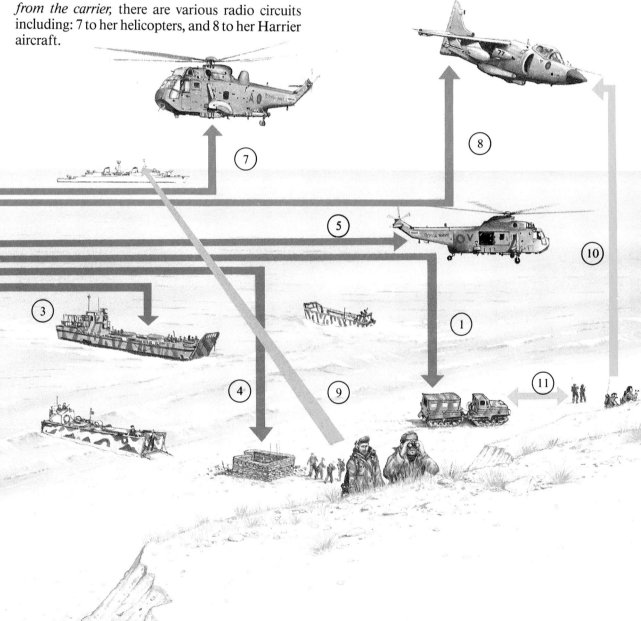

3 Commando Helicopters

Helicopter Carriers

Helicopters (helos) are an ideal means of taking men, guns, stores, and light vehicles from ships to the shore, for helos can fly their cargoes over cliff tops, coastal swamps, and other difficult country. LPH (Landing Platform Helicopter) carriers like the USS *Iwo Jima* (18,300 tons) shown here can also carry Sea Harriers to protect the Assault Ships and support the troops making a landing.

Assault Role — being slow fliers, the helos of an amphibious force do not fly near enemy anti-aircraft defenses, but they can land between 12 and 20 marines in a few seconds, the men sliding down a rope from the hovering aircraft.

Logistic (supply) Role — as a helo can lift an underslung load as well as carry men and supplies in its fuselage, it may land loads which would be difficult to carry ashore in landing craft. Here a Sea King brings a Rapier missile launcher ashore and sets it down on a hilltop. Later in the landings, this flying "truck" will be used to bring ashore urgently-needed ammunition and other combat stores.

Teeny Weenies — light helicopters, like the Royal Marines' Lynx and Gazelle helicopters shown here, may fly at night from ships to scout an enemy coast. At other times, they carry urgently-needed ammunition forward to the artillery and bring back casualties.

4
Assault Craft

The LCVP Coxswain

Corporal Will Derby, as the coxs'n of an LCVP, has a crew of two. One marine is responsible for the engine and the other mans the craft's machine gun. The 30 marines may climb aboard while the craft is still on its parent ship's davits; or they may climb down nets as shown in the picture (bottom left). The smaller craft is very vulnerable at this time, as there is always the danger that a large wave might smash it against the towering sides of the parent ship. Will Derby, therefore, likes to load and get away as quickly as possible.

Having unhooked the craft from the davits' falls (ropes), he steers the craft to circle off the parent ship's bow. Then, when the rest of the flotilla has been loaded, they all follow the flotilla officer's craft some 5 miles (8 km) toward the beach. When they are 1 mile (2 km) or thereabouts from the shore, they pass a control boat moored to show the LCVPs where they must move into line abreast. This they do at a signal from the officer.

Will Derby must keep his craft level with the others either side of him: if he lands his marines ahead of the rest, they will be an easy target for enemy machine gunners. When all the LCVPs hit the beach at the same time, the enemy has too many targets to stop the marines from landing.

The LCU Coxswain

The sergeant coxs'n of an LC Utility has a larger and more complicated craft than Derby's LCVP. The illustration opposite shows the main controls of the LCU. Although it has some accommodation for the crew, they do not normally live aboard.

The sergeant's crew — Royal Marines in British LCUs but sailors in the navies of most other nations — consists of a bowman, a sternsheets man, and a stoker-mechanic. The two deck hands look after the bow and stern mooring ropes, help to unload the craft, and, when not in action, renew ropes and generally maintain the craft in working order. LCU crews can read Morse code sent by lamp. They know what various buoys indicate and understand the flag signals used in amphibious assaults. They also have an elementary knowledge of radio communication circuits.

Klaxon

Compass dimmer

Port & starboard hydraulic oil pressures

Phone

Helm angle

Binnacle

Port & starboard throttle

Compass

Generator

Phone socket

Yodel alarm

Dimmer

UHF/VHF radio

Dimmer

Aldis box

Cable tensioner

Freefall control

Port RPM

Starboard RPM

Ramp control

Emergency engine stops

Engine oil pressure

LC Utility — the workhorse of the modern amphibious fleet

5
The Men of the Landing Force

British Royal Marine
American Marine

The Royal Marine commando (on the left) in his green beret carries his Self-Loading Rifle and all the equipment and rations he may need for several days ashore. In his Bergen rucksack is his spare clothing, his rations, a small cooker, and waterproof jacket and trousers. His sleeping bag may be hitched to his rucksack, and he will probably carry his section of the 10-man tent used when the men are not in action.

Rolled up under the flap of his rucksack is a polystyrene sleeping mat; this keeps his sleeping bag insulated from damp ground. His steel helmet can be seen slung from his rucksack, and the top of the Carl Gustav anti-tank weapon shows above the rucksack. Its cover prevents water getting into the barrel as he wades ashore and will keep out any dirt as he carries it to the battle area.

When going into action, his heavy weapon is carried on a sling over the shoulder, ready to be fired (see right). Fired from the shoulder, it can damage, if not stop, a tank at 150 feet (450m) with a special round. At other times it may be used to fire explosive 84mm rounds or smoke rounds up to a 3300 feet (1000m). It can also fire parachute flares 6600 feet (2000m) into the air to light up a battlefield.

Other commandos will carry radios (see picture right) while many carry 81mm mortar bombs on to the mortar men. Each man will leave his two or three bombs with the mortar teams as the Sections move towards a forming up position where they will assemble ready to put in an attack.

Amphibious attack

The Marine's heavy pack and sleeping bag will be left in a pile some distance away from the forming up area. In the case of the first companies ashore, these heavier pieces of kit will be left in the commando ship. During the fighting to establish the beachhead or in later battles, the Marines may have to live for several days without their sleeping bags or a change of clothing. At such times, their tough training pays off, for less well trained troops cannot stay fighting fit in such rough conditions.

In action a man might have to use his knife or bayonet, will certainly have to cross open ground as

British Royal Marine

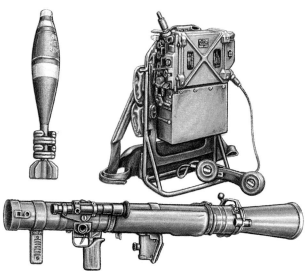

Full kit

The illustrations show the equipment a Royal Marine commando or a United States Marine might carry when landing in the second or third wave. They are trained to carry such heavy kits because, unlike ordinary infantry, they will have to march on a beachhead where few vehicles can be landed. Before going into action, they will stack their packs and bedrolls and pass the mortar bombs on to the mortar men. Then, carrying the same kit as the assault waves came ashore with, these Marines will be ready for action.

quickly as possible and may need to climb rock cliffs or other obstacles. At such times, he must be as lightly equipped as possible and carry only ammunition, grenades, and a few emergency rations.

The Assault Waves

The men landed in the first wave of LCVPs or helicopters carry only essentials (see US Marine — far right). They have their weapons, ammunition, radios, emergency rations, and drinking water. But how much ammunition should they take? How long may they be ashore before more ammunition can be landed for them?

These are difficult questions to answer because if they carry too much ammunition, especially mortar bombs which are heavy, the LCVPs will be overloaded. Then, low in the water, they may fill and sink in even a moderately rough sea, as waves slop into the boat. Alternatively, if there are fewer men, each carrying heavier loads, there may be a risk of not landing enough men to win the battle ashore. The answer is always a compromise, with probably fewer men and less ammunition than the commander would like in the first wave.

Bed rolls, spare clothing, and their full rations are landed for the assault troops once the force has established a beachhead.

American Marine

6 Tracked Landing Vehicles

Landing craft and helos provide little or no armor plate to protect the men they are carrying ashore. The men also have to cross the shallow water between the landing craft's ramp and the shore, called the "water gap." In wading this, they may be slowed in their dash for cover and will certainly get wet feet. This is only a discomfort in most climates, but it is very dangerous in arctic conditions where men can get cold-weather injuries like frostbite.

The Alligator

The picture top right shows one of the first Mark I Landing Vehicles, Tracked (LVTs), which climbed ashore at Tulgai in the Pacific to land US Marines in 1942. The picture shows clearly the blades of the tracks which drove this LVT through calm water.

Its main drawback was that the gunners were dangerously exposed to enemy bullets as they stood firing over the bow.

A number of improved types of LVTs came from this early amphibian that could move at 4 mph (6 km/h) over water and 15 mph (25 km/h) over land. Later types had a door-ramp at the back so that having crawled across the beach to the safety of the dunes, the LVT could disgorge its 24 riflemen into cover from enemy fire.

The LVT Personnel 7 A1

Early LVTs were open-topped and, therefore, the marines to be landed, the cargo personnel, were vulnerable to the plunging fire of mortar bombs or shells bursting in the air above the LVT. The cargo personnel in landing craft may also be wounded by air-burst high explosive shells. By the 1960s, the men in LVTs were totally enclosed in the Mark 7 LVT by aluminium armor (bottom left). This LVT is driven by two water-jets when afloat, the jets being moved by deflection plates to steer the LVT to the beach at 8 mph (13 km/h). If the jets fail to work, its tracks still give it a speed of just over 4 mph (7 km/h).

Armored Amphibians

Some early LVTs were fitted with turrets for flame-throwers and M-6 37mm guns or M-8 75mm

LVT P7A1 with machine gun cupola and completely covered cargo-personnel compartment

howitzers. As LVT (Armored), these swam ashore before the first wave of LVTs carrying marine infantry. The LVT(A)s, firing like tanks, could then destroy beach defenses.

In the 1970s, the LVT Howitzer (LVTH) was used by the US Marines, but it is likely to be replaced by air-cushion or hovercraft, described later.

Waterproofing

Almost any vehicle can be made waterproof. But if it is to swim as opposed to wading, it must have water-jets or propellers. Otherwise, when it floats free, it may be swept away by the tide. Many types of armored vehicle are waterproofed, but they can only wade.

Alligator amphibious "amtrack," an LVT Mark 1, swimming in 1942

LVT (Armored) Mark 1 with a 37mm M-6 gun in a turret of 12.75mm armor plate

German amphibious ½-ton truck, the GAZ-48 MAV. Note the propellers.

7
Special Forces

These elite forces include the American Navy's Seal Teams of swimmers, the Royal Marines' Special Boat Squadron, the SBS, and the British Army's Special Air Service, the SAS. They each have teams trained in reconnaissance, with the Seal Teams and SBS specializing in beach recces.

The swimmers are landed secretly some days, or even weeks, before the landing force. In the Falklands, SAS and SBS teams were ashore for three weeks before the commandos and paratroopers came ashore on May 21, 1982. During this time, they made some beach recces and answered a number of important questions for the Landing Force commanders.

Some of the questions were common to all recces before a battle. How strong is the enemy, and where are the enemy's defenses? Are there any swamps or streams or other natural obstacles which might slow down advancing troops?

The commander of any amphibious force needs to know the answers to other questions. Are there any strong tidal currents running past the beach which might set the LCVPs off course? Are there any hidden shallows where a sandbar lies off the beach? If there are, the landing craft will be caught on them and then, as men and vehicles drive off the craft, they may have to pass through deep water to reach the shore, exposing men to the risk of drowning. If the water is deep, but not deep enough to drown them, the men will only be able to move slowly through the water, making them an easy target for enemy machine gunners.

The slope of the shore — its incline — must be suitable for landing-craft. If it is too gentle, the craft's propellers may hit the sand before the boat is near the water's edge. In this case, the marines will have a long way to run through water to reach the beach. If the incline is too steep, the crew of the craft will have difficulty getting the bow firmly on

A

A. A surface swimmer of 1944 with a fishing line on the reel fixed to his belt (see B right). On his right wrist is a watertight watch, or he might wear a waterproof compass there. On his left sleeve is a slate for noting depths or other details with a special China marking pencil.

the shore. An ideal beach has a slope which enables the craft to put its bow firmly on the shore while its propellers at the stern are still floating clear of the sand.

The proposed beachhead must also have paths, preferably wide ones, leading from the shore inland. These beach exits are needed so tanks and other vehicles can be driven clear of the beach. Obviously, high cliffs behind a beach are a problem for the landing force, but even low cliffs can be difficult to cross, even though they may not appear difficult when seen on aerial photographs.

The swimmers also take samples of sand and gravel. These are then checked to see if the ground is firm enough to carry beach roadways. Bad patches must be avoided by LVTs because some stones may jam their tracks or they may slide about on a thin layer of clay lying over rock.

B. In 1944 the swimmer measured the depth of water every 7 feet (2m) as he played out his line. The intervals were marked by lead pellets he could feel on the line. The weighted line he lowered had pellets every 12 inches (30cm).

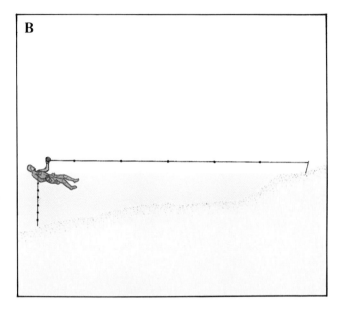

C. In the 1980s a swimmer may parachute to a submarine that carries him to near the enemy shore. Then he swims ashore and may cut out plugs of sand with an auger for later examination to see if it will carry the weight of a vehicle.

8 Amphibious Raids and Raiding

It may be advantageous for raids into enemy territory to be made from the sea for several reasons. A team may land with explosives to sabotage a railway line, used to take men and supplies to the main battle, or they may place mines on enemy roads. Such raids force the enemy to bring in troops from the main battle area to protect these supply routes.

Seaborne raiders have also sabotaged coal mines, factories producing war materials like aluminum, and enemy oil wells. But their usual job is to land a few hours before the main assault to knock out enemy radar, missiles, and coast guns. The amphibious ships can then anchor more safely off the coast.

At other times, raiders may land to leave false information. In such deception raids, they might leave a damaged inflatable dinghy on the shore. With it would be maps and, perhaps, some misleading written orders, all suggesting that this particular beach was an intended landing point. The enemy will then reinforce his defenses there. The swimmers making the recce of the true landing points must be careful not to be caught; nor must they leave behind any sign that they have made a recce. Otherwise, the main landing force could meet strong resistance.

A. Canoeists use double paddles for speed. But when inside any enemy harbor, these are each divided into four single paddles. A man with a single paddle can then move the canoe with stealth, and there is no flash of the blades to alert sentries.

A

To reduce the chance of being detected on landing, the canoeists choose the spot where they will come ashore very carefully. Preferably, the landing place would be near a rocky outcrop or, in the tropics, by a patch of mangrove trees. They also prefer to land where there is a gentle ripple of waves, as these tend to break up the eddies made by the paddles. Ideally, they will make a landing when there is no moon.

B. An exercise in daylight for what would be a night landing. Here, they climb a cliff and put two land-based Exocet missiles out of action before they sink assault ships.

The Rendezvous

After a beach reconnaissance, the canoeists must bring out their sand samples and the details of depths of water off the beach. Therefore, one man usually stays in the canoe. This paddler can then launch the swimmer about 300 feet (100m) from the beach before taking the canoe further out to sea where it is unlikely to be noticed, especially if he keeps the bow pointing towards the coast. This makes a small silhouette.

At a pre-arranged time and place, he paddles back inshore to collect the swimmer who swims out to meet him. During World War II, he would have carried a hooded torch with which to flash a Morse code letter that the paddler would recognize as a signal from his friend. Once picked up, the swimmer would help to paddle back to the submarine as quickly as possible.

In World War II, the submarine would flash an infrared signal only visible to the canoeist with special equipment. In more recent times, the canoeists reach the RV (rendezvous) area and use a bongle. The submarine picks up the underwater noise this makes and zeroes in on the canoe.

If the canoeists fail to meet the submarine at the first RV, there is a second one pre-arranged for a later time further offshore. If that fails, an emergency RV will be set for the following and later nights.

C. Two stages in the rendezvous (RV) between the swimmer and his paddler and their canoe with its parent submarine

9
The Greatest Assault Force in History

The "Overlord" Landings in Normandy, France, on June 6, 1944

1 American, British, and Canadian armies were led ashore by naval and army engineers clearing mines and obstructions.
2 The assault engineers were supported by "swimming" tanks with propellers and canvas screens that enabled them to float.
3 Assault companies of soldiers were landed from US Navy LCVPs and Royal Marine LC Assault.

Key

beach obstacles

engineers

swimming tanks

LCVP/LCAs

LCTs carrying tanks

LCTs carrying tanks

LCG (L)

LCFs

LCT (Rocket)

LCA (Hedgerow)

LCT carrying self-propelled guns

LCM

Destroyer

LCI (Small)

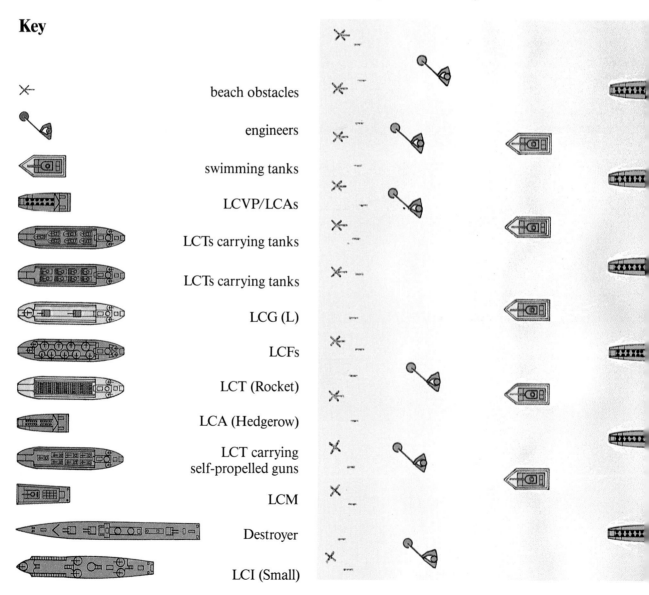

4 Landing craft with 4.7-inch naval guns, LC gun (Large), and light anti-aircraft guns, LC Flak, gave close support to the assault waves from the flanks.

5 LC Tank fitted with rockets as LCT(R) and LCA (Hedgerow) with spigot mortars fired at the beach to cut lanes through mines and wire.

6 LCTs brought in tanks including Royal Marine Centaurs to support the assault companies and tanks with concrete-busting mortars manned by Royal Engineers.

7 Other LCTs carried self-propelled artillery, fired at the beach on the run-in.

8 The early build-up of men and stores was made by LC Mechanized (today LCUs) and by large troop-carrying landing craft, the LC Infantry (Large).

9 Warships and planes bombarded the defenses for several hours before the landings.

Note: Many other special craft, large and small, ferried supplies to the beaches, laid smoke screens, controlled the assault waves, and even provided kitchens on the beach. There were over 6,800 ships and craft in these landings.

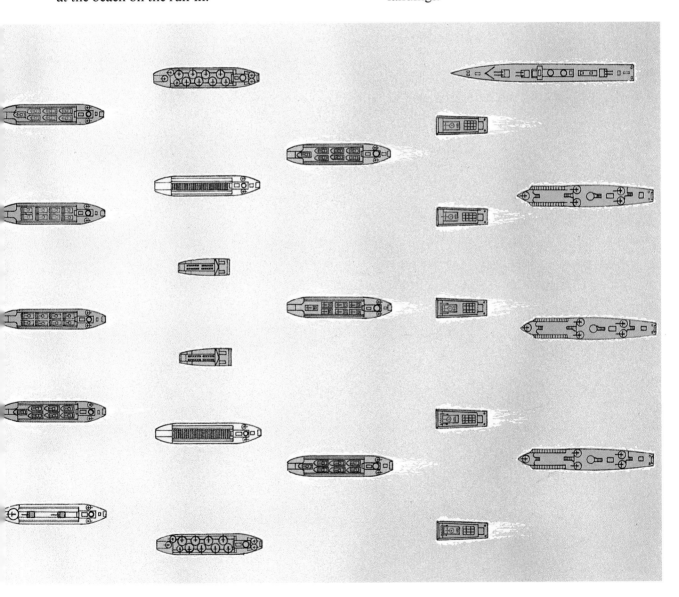

10 Amphibious Warfare in the Pacific

Pacific Distances

Between 1942 and 1945, the American amphibious forces captured islands from the Solomons to Japan, a distance of over 3,300 miles (5,500km), nearly equal to that from North America to England. For such long voyages, they needed Landing Ships rather than Landing Craft.

Assault on Iwo Jima

The US Navy and American aircraft bombarded this island south of Japan for ten weeks before the landings. D-Day (the day of the landings) here was February 19, 1945, and the H-hour (the time the first assault wave hit the beach) was 9:00 AM. The ships had sailed over 450 miles (750km) from their bases in islands to the south.

Converted LCIs drenched the defenses with rockets for an hour and a half before H-hour. Then 68 LVT(A)s led in 482 LVTs carrying marines of the 4th and 5th Divisions.

The battle lasted seven weeks because the Japanese had deep underground bunkers on this island, which is only about 4 by 2½ miles (7km by 4km). 6,812 US marines and sailors were killed in these battles, and over 18,000 Japanese died in the defenses. Iwo Jima had some of the strangest defense bunkers ever built: the natural caves on the island were reinforced with steel and concrete—a nightmare of defenses for assault engineers trying to destroy them.

A. Iwo Jima is an extinct volcano in which the Japanese had deep bunkers. Passages from these ran to the surface, where guns were firing at the US ships.

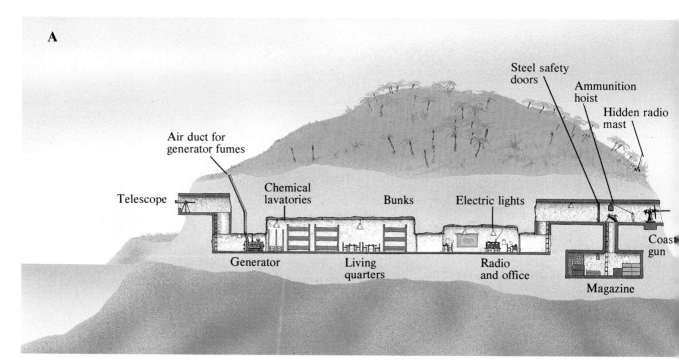

A

Telescope · Air duct for generator fumes · Chemical lavatories · Bunks · Electric lights · Steel safety doors · Ammunition hoist · Hidden radio mast · Coast gun · Generator · Living quarters · Radio and office · Magazine

Other Landings

The US Marines had fought in a series of amphibious operations to reach Iwo Jima. By February 1945 they were a well-practiced assault force with the naval warships and landing craft of American task forces, including the rocket ships (see picture). Other support craft included the LCS (Large) mark 3 with a dual purpose 3-inch/50, able to fire at high angles against aircraft or at low angles against shore defenses. The craft also had two twin-Bofors 40mm guns. Other craft had three 4½-inch (114mm) mortars, and all carried several light anti-aircraft weapons.

After the landings on Iwo Jima, a major landing was made on Okinawa on April 1, 1945. This large island, less then 360 miles (600km) from Japan, was heavily fortified. But the 183,000 men in 1,300 vessels met little opposition on the beach, as the Japanese had moved inland to avoid the naval bombardment. The island was captured after fourteen weeks of hard fighting in major land battles.

C. The LSTs launched the amphibian LVTs into the water some 3 miles (4.5 km) from the beach.

B. The Landing Ship Medium (Rocket) launched rockets each 127mm in diameter, and some LSM (R)s which could launch 1,040 of these in a minute, but needed 45 minutes to reload.

11 Assault Engineers in Amphibious Operations

Beach Defenses

The picture shows some of the Germans' defenses on the Normandy beaches in 1944. They were built along the tide line and were covered by the sea when the tide was in. Many of the defenses had mines or old shells fixed to them so that they would explode if struck by a landing craft. Therefore, the mines and obstructions had to be removed to provide clear paths to the shore, some 165 feet (50m) wide. Landing craft could then beach without the risk of being holed and sunk by the obstacles.

Landing Craft Obstruction Clearance Units and Underwater Demolition Teams

British (LCOCU) and American (UDT) swimmers, who were also shallow water divers, cleared paths to the beach. It was a difficult job. The largest obstacle, the "Belgian Gate" (see picture), needed 36 small charges of explosive to break up its heavy steel frames.

Above the Tide Line

Barbed wire and mines were laid to prevent assault troops from reaching the concrete bunkers at the back of the beaches. These mines and the wire had to be cleared by army engineers, who also came ashore in special tanks on the British beaches. These tanks, Assault Vehicles Royal Engineers, had a variety of unusual weapons. One fired a "concrete bursting" mortar bomb the size of a garbage can. This could stun the men in a pillbox or bunker even when it did not break through the 10 to 13 feet (3-4 meters) of concrete wall.

Conventional Defenses

Offshore minefields had to be swept as in any naval operation, but in Normandy the coast guns had to be knocked out before the minesweepers could operate.

Ashore, flail tanks cleared paths through mines laid behind the beach. As in many battles, flamethrower tanks and bridging tanks (able to place a bridge across a 33 feet (10 m) ditch) were used. In any amphibious landing, as in Normandy in 1944, these special tanks must be carried to the battle in ships, put ashore, and often brought into action with little or no cover from hills or folds in the ground, for beaches tend to be flat and open.

Landing Berths

As in the Pacific, to bring ashore all the tanks, vehicles, and men required in the build-up at Normandy, landing ships were used. Before these could beach, however, engineers had to dig out berths in the sand or coral. This was a job for armor-plated bulldozers.

12 Landing Tanks on a Beach

The Idea

In 1941 Sir Winston Churchill wanted ships that could land tanks on a beach and, being Prime Minister at the time, he was able to arrange for them to be designed. The majority were built in America to a British design. The size of a ferry boat, these ships had a displacement of over 4,000 tons. Still, they required only about three feet of water to float their bows onto a beach. They could carry 500 tons of supplies when beaching and had a crew of 7 officers and 204 men. Despite the shallow water in which they landed, there was often a wide water-gap to the dry land. Although this was covered in part by the ramp they lowered when the bow doors were open, various methods were tried to bridge this gap. The most successful was to float a pontoon from the shore to the LST's ramp.

By the end of the Second World War, there were several types of Landing Ships. The Landing Ship Medium, being 3 knots faster than an LST, was able to sail with a 12-knot convoy. The Landing Ship Vehicle could carry 44 DUKWs—pronounced "ducks"—the main amphibious truck of the Second World War, with 800 troops.

Landing Tanks from Shore to Shore

During the Second World War, there were several types of LC Tank. Smaller than an LST, they were nevertheless able to load in a friendly port, sail more than a hundred miles, and land their tanks straight on to a beach. The smallest of these

An American Newport-class Landing Ship Tank

LCTs, the Mark 5s and 6s, could be carried on the deck of an LST and were launched by heeling the ship in sheltered waters.

LSTs from the Second World War were in operations in Korea, the landings at Port Said, Egypt, and elsewhere in the 1950s.

Landing Ships in the 1980s

In the late 1960s, the US Navy began to use a larger and faster LST, the "Newport" class (see picture). Able to cruise at 20 knots, these ships have solid bows without doors, so they land their tanks or other heavy vehicles over an aluminum ramp 11 feet (33m) long. This ramp is carried over the bow by two great derrick arms. The ship can also launch LVTs or load LCUs through its stern gate.

The Russians have a class of LST, the "Alligators" of 4,100 tons, with ramps and bow doors. Their much larger "Rogov" class of 13,000 tons (see picture) can land vehicles through a stern gate, just as car-ferries load and offload.

Although these LSTs can make 20 knots, they are vulnerable to air attack, and their crews humorously call them "Long Slow Targets." They have to be protected by escorting warships, and it is a question of how many such escorts are available that will decide the extent of any amphibious invasions in the future.

LSTs have to set out for their target beaches some days, if not weeks, before a landing. This approach voyage, with the hazards of air and submarine attack, may also reveal the invaders' intentions, especially now that satellites can track the passage of a convoy toward a hostile coast. The Americans, therefore, keep some ships loaded with transport and combat supplies in areas where there may be need for an amphibious landing.

The Royal Marines have also solved the problem of the time it takes to carry vehicles from the United Kingdom to Norway. They keep ready a number of their oversnow vehicles and other heavy equipment in Norway.

A Russian Rogov-class landing ship, with stern gate and bow door

13 Beach Masters, Forward Operating Bases, and Other Developments

Royal Marine Beach Parties

Like all other amphibious forces, the British land men trained to control traffic over a beach. This involves marines in directing vehicles from the landing points to the beach exits, calling in LCUs and LSTs to their landing berths (see picture bottom left), and may also involve the control of helos to an LZ (Landing Zone) in the beachhead.

The Beach Master is in charge of all movement across and from the beach. His party of men help LC crews to move a stranded or sinking craft. They also tow clear of the water any vehicles bogged down in a water gap by means of a Beach Armored Recovery Vehicle, BARV (see picture top right).

Forward Operating Bases

Once the beachhead is established, landing craft can be more easily serviced ashore than in their parent ships. A forward base is therefore set up to repair engines and hull damage. The craft may be hauled clear of the water on a makeshift slipway so that propellers and rudders can be repaired or replaced easily.

Beach Roadways

Engineers lay steel mesh strips from the landing berths to the nearest coast road. These strips form beach roadways that prevent vehicles from becoming bogged down in the beachhead.

Air-cushion (hover) craft

The LC Air Cushion needs no roadway and can land on beaches where other landing craft cannot work because of offshore reefs or marshy ground near the coast. The American LCAC in the picture (center right) is about the size of an LCU but can be used on many more stretches of coast. It carries men and supplies at over 60 mph (100 km/h), and takes only 20 minutes to come ashore from a parent ship lying 18 miles (30 km) from the beach. Its use may completely change present ideas of initial landings in waves with a subsequent build-up across a beach, for the LCAC can carry its cargo well inland.

The Russians use several types of air-cushion craft, including the large "Aist" in the picture (bottom right). This sails from land bases in the Baltic, avoiding the necessity of building large parent ships to carry big hovercraft across oceans.

Left: Beach Master's party signals in craft to berths marked by cloth banners and lights

top: The BARV, manned by Royal Marines, tows a "drowned" vehicle clear of the water.

center: An impression of an American LC Air Cushion

below: A Russian Aist air-cushion craft lands 150 men and 5 armored vehicles after coming ashore at 42 mph (70 km/h).

31

14 Landing Combat Stores

The weight of combat stores

A modern brigade may use over 200 tons of ammunition and other combat supplies (rations of food, gasoline, and drinking water) each day, enough to fill 50 large trucks. If the brigade's artillery are in action, too, they might need another 20 tons.

To get such quantities to a beachhead, both ferry craft—shuttling to and from ships anchored off the beach—and LST-type ships to offload cargoes straight onto the beach are required.

Ferry work

The British land supplies on large pontoon barges, Mexefloats, which are manned by the Royal Corps of Transport. Each ferry can carry ten or more loaded 4-ton trucks. These drive off the pontoon onto a beach roadway (see picture B).

LCUs are used mainly for landing supplies and can tow ashore a Dracone. This is a very large sausage-shaped skin filled with fuel and officially described as "a flexible barge" (see picture A). Fuel for aircraft, tanks, trucks, generators, and other motorized equipment is pumped from the Dracone into storage tanks ashore. One of the many complications of handling combat supplies is that the Landing Force uses several different fuels. These must each be brought ashore and stored separately because the ordinary gasoline used in trucks cannot be used in aircraft that need Avcat (aviation fuel).

There are several types of LCU. Some are twice the size of the Royal Navy's ferry craft. These large LCUs of the US Navy can each land three M-103 tanks and are not unlike the smaller LCTs of the 1940s.

A. The Landing Craft Utility here is towing a "flexible fuel barge" Dracone, which may be filled with aircraft fuel or other fuel. Having landed its two tanks in an assault, the LCU will then provide a ferry service from supply ships to the beachhead.

A

Logistic Landing Ships

Each of these British ships can carry eight days' combat supplies for a Commando Unit with its supporting artillery battery and troop of engineers. As in the LST, vehicles move from deck to deck along ramps as in a multistory parking ramp. When they reach the main deck, which runs from the bow ramp to the stern gate, they may be driven ashore. With the bow doors open (see picture C) or

---

C. The landing Ship Logistic of the RN Reserve can offload stores twice as fast as merchant ships.

B. A Mexefloat raft can ferry vehicles ashore in calm conditions.

---

an LCU hitched on at the stern gate, vehicles can be landed straight onto the beach or ferried ashore.

Floating Roadways

At Normandy in 1944, two large floating harbors, called "Mulberries," were sunk off the beaches and linked to them by a floating road. In the 1980s, similar pontoon causeways can be positioned by Warping Tugs, which can also lay fuel pipes from ships anchored offshore to storage tanks on the beachhead.

15
Fire Support

Naval Gunfire

The destroyer HMS *Antrim* with her twin 114 mm guns is seen in the picture (below left) bombarding a target that her gunners cannot see. They have received directions about where to aim from a Royal Artillery officer who is ashore. This Forward Observer (FO) has been landed secretly behind the main enemy defenses. Once ashore, his radio operator sets up a link with the ship, sending the FO's directions over the radio in Morse code (below right).

The target may be a well-camouflaged bunker or a road which the enemy are using. The ship's gunners aim at the target using instruments. Having done some sums, they know roughly which settings are needed on the instruments to aim the guns. But their first shot may be wide of the target.

The FO sees this and sends a radio message, giving the adjustments necessary to hit the target with the second shot.

All the FO's messages must be brief and in cypher (A=E, D=P or whatever). Otherwise, the enemy may not only understand the message but pinpoint where the FO has his radio, for they will have radio operators listening for such signals.

Air Support

Also secretly ashore are Forward Air Controllers. They are in radio contact with pilots of the Harrier or other aircraft supporting the landing force. They work in ways similar to the Naval Gunfire Forward Observer. Speaking over his radio, the FAC describes the position of a target as "100m north of the road junction, in the wood to the east of the road," for example.

At other times, the aircraft will circle high over a battlefield, ready to answer the FAC's call to strike a particular target.

The advancing marines may call on either the FAC or the Naval Gunfire Forward Observer to bring down fire on any enemy position the marines

HMS Antrim fires at a shore target

The Forward Observer and his radio operator directing naval gunfire onto a target

cannot crack. But neither gunfire nor missiles nor bombs can be fired from the aircraft if the targets are too close to the marines. Despite what is often written about the accuracy of modern weapons, most of the fighting has still to be done with old fashioned shells, rockets, and bombs.

Such fire support is essential in the early stages of a landing, as the Commando artillery cannot be set up ashore with their 105mm light guns until a beachhead is secured. Therefore, the FOs and FACs go ashore with the first assault troops — if they have not been landed before.

When the defenders of a coastline are not too strongly established inland, FOs and FACs may be landed in secret. They can then hide by day while looking for suitable targets, and the FOs will control night shoots by warships.

The warships approach the enemy coast after dark, because their radios can be detected by an enemy's electronic equipment, they keep radio silence. Then, at the appointed time, the ships open their radio circuits and receive directions from the FO ashore. He will give them a reference for the first target, which they can then find on a map. Knowing exactly where they have to aim, they open fire on the guns' control instruments, after making the various settings for its range and so on.

As the first round drops, the FO can see if it is short, over, or wide of the target. He then radios a correction to increase the range or whatever. The gunners re-set their instruments and fire again. Once shots start hitting the target, the guns will fire continuously until it is destroyed. The FO then radios to cease fire.

All the time he is ashore, the FO is in danger of being detected by the enemy, and his radio signals could give him away. Because the enemy has equipment which will detect where his signals are coming from, he must keep them very brief. Special radios are made which send such signals in short, sharp bursts, making them hard to detect and locate.

A harrier responds to a Forward Air Controller's request for a strike against ground targets.

16 Improvisations

No navy can afford to have sufficient ships to land a large force, and so civilian merchant ships are pressed into service in wartime. In the Second World War, many hundreds of such ships were used to carry landing craft in place of their lifeboats. More complicated changes had to be made to the civilian ships used in the landings on the Falkland Islands in 1982.

Container Ships

The US Navy has produced a set of prefabricated parts that will change a *Seawitch* container ship into a small aircraft carrier. In peacetime, equipment is stored. When war is expected, however, it takes only one day to fit it over the deck of a container ship.

The ship may then carry helicopters for the landing force or Sea Harriers. A squadron of the Harriers on two or three ships can fly off them to support the assault waves. Later they will move to a shore base, and the container ship can offload the combat stores in her holds.

Ships for the Falkland Islands

The liner *Canberra* was converted into a Landing Ship Luxury Liner (LSLL) by adding helicopter flight decks over the swimming pool areas, the only part of her superstructure strong enough for the job. The Roll-on-Roll-off (Ro-Ro) North Sea Ferry *Norland* was given flight decks also. Her stern gate arrangements, normally used to offload cars and trucks at a special dockside, could be easily adapted for Mexefloats. Then Mexefloats and LCUs could be coupled up to her stern and vehicles driven off *Norland* onto the craft.

Other Improvisations

While many other ships were being modified for use in the South Atlantic, the landing forces were improvising too. For example, M Company of 42 Commando Royal Marines was embarked in the supply ship *Tidespring* to take them to South Georgia. This island, over 720 miles (1,200 km) east-south-east of the Falklands, had been occupied by Argentinians. Before the company could land, however, the Royal Marine major in command had to land 75 men from HMS *Antrim*. With the support of naval gunfire, these men, who came from several different units, forced 137 Argentinians to surrender.

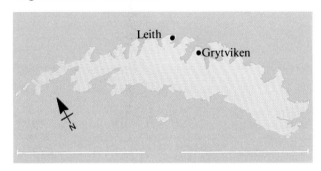

Leith
Grytviken

South Georgia, over 90 miles (1500 km) east of the Falkland Islands, was recaptured in April 1982.

Right: The prefabricated parts which convert a *Seawitch* container ship into a small aircraft carrier include: a hangar roof and workshops (blue), living accommodation (yellow), the flight deck (green). All these are fitted forward of the superstructure and over containers of combat stores in the hull spaces (sand color). Aft are the fuel tanks, also in prefabricated containers (lilac), over which fits a container-type housing (brick red) with equipment for pumping fuel into the aircraft. This self-contained unit, like the others, can be lowered by a dockside crane ready to be securely fixed as a part of the ship.

In the 1980s, British and American Marines have a number of ways in which they might make arrangements to reduce the extent of improvisations in an emergency. These are usually ways and means of storing prefabricated equipment which — like the *Seawitch* carrier kit — can be slotted onto a merchant ship.

Containers are of standard sizes and made to nest together, which is a considerable help in preparing for such conversions of cargo ships to assault ships.

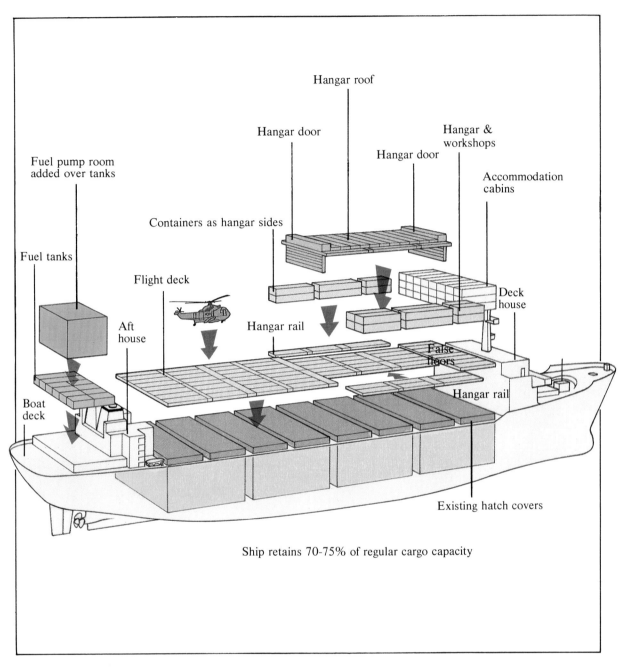

Fuel pump room
added over tanks

Fuel tanks

Flight deck

Aft
house

Boat
deck

Containers as hangar sides

Hangar door

Hangar roof

Hangar door

Hangar &
workshops

Accommodation
cabins

Hangar rail

Deck
house

False
floors

Hangar rail

Existing hatch covers

Ship retains 70-75% of regular cargo capacity

A container may be fitted with anti-aircraft guns, ship-to-shore radios, and a host of other military items, all ready to drop into place on a merchant ship in an emergency.

Another precaution, which will save time in an emergency and go part way to avoid improvised fittings on a ship, is to build ships with extra strong decks. Decks must be strengthened only where a flight deck is to be fitted or guns mounted, but if this can be done while the ship is being built — as was the practice for British ships in the 1930s — then she can be converted to an assault ship in days rather than weeks.

The difficulty with all such preparations is that they cost a lot of money and require keeping ready kits that may never actually be used. Therefore, amphibious forces are often short of the right type of vessels when a war starts.

17
The Landings at San Carlos

In April 1982 the Argentinians occupied the British Falklands. A landing force was then sent over 7,800 miles (13,000 km) from Britain to retake the islands. They began their campaign by establishing a beachhead at San Carlos (see diagram map).

Why San Carlos? The senior officers commanding the landing force (3 Commando Brigade) and their assault ships wanted to land where there were few, if any, Argentinian beach defenses. The commanders also wanted to anchor their ships as far as possible from the Argentine airfields on the islands, as this would limit air attacks while the landings were being made.

San Carlos could also be defended more easily than other possible beachheads. As soon as the commandos and paratroopers were on the hills surrounding this anchorage, with Rapier anti-aircraft missile launchers also in place, they could prevent the Argentinians driving them back into the sea.

The plan was to put ashore Commando units and Paratrooper battalions by landing craft, as shown in the diagram picture. Before this, an Argentinian outpost on Fanning Head had to be captured. Otherwise, aircraft and Exocet missile attacks might be directed by men in the outpost against the amphibious ships. Marines of the Special Boat Squadron were landed by helicopter to take out this post, which they did in a sharp little battle.

Then the marines moved back to San Carlos to set up landing lights to guide in the landing craft, including several LCUs with light-armored vehicles in their bows. This armor could give them some close support fire as "a poor man's LC Gun."

The landing force came ashore in the dark, which gave them a good chance of surprising the Argentinians and several hours of cover in which to set up defenses against counter-attacks. In the assault, there were some delays in getting the troops ashore, but none serious enough to prevent the marines and paratroopers capturing several beachheads by daylight that morning, May 21. The only British casualties were three marines killed when their light helicopters were shot down. By that Friday night, the small beachheads of the morning had been joined together into one large one.

In the following days, despite brave attacks by Argentinian pilots, the marines and paratroopers broke out of the beachhead. They were to fight several battles, but by June 14 they had forced the Argentinians to surrender.

Night Attacks

The first attack was made by 2 para moving south from the beachhead towards Goose Green. They had intended to destroy aircraft on the airstrip there and withdraw. But after coming under heavy fire around dawn on May 26, they fought their way against great odds to the airstrip. It was an action in which their Commanding Officer, Lt.-Col. H. Jones, won a posthumous VC, and his men achieved a great victory. Meanwhile, the Commandos climbed over the mountains and, on the night of June 11-12, put in two skillful night attacks.

45 Commando attacked the Two Sisters, formidable rock crags rising 66 feet (20m) above an open mountainside. From these crags, the Argentinian machine gunners could fire into a great valley bowl north of the mountain. Here about a mile (2km) from the crags, 45 Commando's Y and Z Companies formed up. Meanwhile, X Company moved around to the south to attack the western Twin.

Although X Company had some delays, all three Companies advanced in arrowhead formation. They were fired on when 825 feet (250m) from the defenses. But once the Commando artillery and mortars had subdued these machine gunners a little, the Marines charged and captured these strong defense positions.

To the south, 42 Commando was attacking Mount Harriet after K Company had made a hazardous march of about $2\frac{1}{2}$ miles (4km) to loop behind the defenses. Advancing silently up the hill not long after midnight, they were within 396 feet (120m) of the defenses before the enemy realized that the commandos were there. L Company had already begun to move up the western slope despite heavy fire. By co-ordinating their attacks using radios between the company commanders, they charged the mountaintop positions.

3 Para in a similar night attack captured Mount Longdon. All three attacks broke the back of the Argentinian defenses.

San Carlos Water in East Falkland Island, where the Reinforced 3 Commando Brigade landed in the early hours of May 21, 1982. Landing craft carried 3 Para (green arrows) to Port San Carlos, 40 Commando and 2 Para (blue) to San Carlos Settlement, and 45 Commando (red) to Ajax Bay.

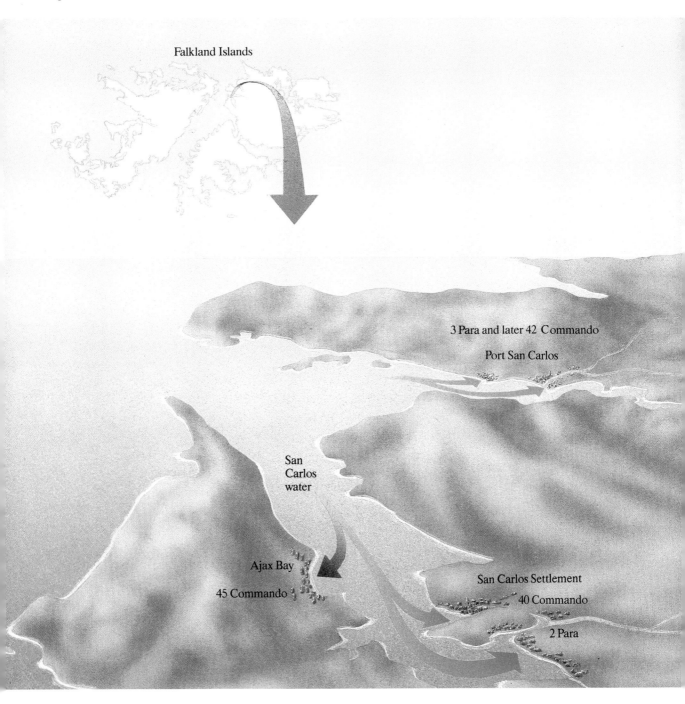

Falkland Islands

3 Para and later 42 Commando

Port San Carlos

San Carlos water

Ajax Bay

45 Commando

San Carlos Settlement

40 Commando

2 Para

18 North of the Arctic Circle

The map here shows the area of north Norway where US Marines, 3 Commando Brigade RM, and the Norwegian army will fight should there ever be a war with Russia. Each January since 1979, the British marines have trained their Commando Brigade in this snow-covered area for three months or more. This was one of the main reasons for the efficient way this Brigade fought in the Falklands.

Men in Combined Operations in this arctic cold need special vehicles. These can only be landed from LCUs which are protected from the cold — as the one in the picture — by a cover built over the vehicle deck. Also shown is a tracked BV 202, which can cross snow at 9 mph (15 km/h), because this over-snow vehicle's broad tracks do not create much more pressure on the ground than does a skier. The skier might well be a Royal Marine commando, for two Commando units are trained to fight on skis.

In such warfare, the commando has to survive in bitter cold. In some ways, this is less difficult than in a thaw, for the cold keeps everything frozen dry. The wind adds to the cold, lowering the temperature several degrees as it disperses the heat of the body. When the wind blows from the west, however, it can be warm enough to thaw ice and snow. Men then have to wear clothing that will keep them dry. For this reason Arctic-trained commandos wear a great variety of clothing.

They wear gloves with mittens over them to avoid frostbite. If a man catches hold of metal with his bare hands he gets "burned," since the cold freezes his skin to the metal. The vehicle mechanic or the raiding craft coxswain must, therefore, wear gloves when working on an engine, as must a driver if he has to change a track on his vehicle.

Special boots are worn that can be used to march along roads or be fitted into the bindings attaching skis to the boots. In some conditions, a commando finds snowshoes — "bear feet" as he calls them — more suitable than skis. Included in his kit are heavy boots. They are designed to keep his feet warm when on watch but are not easy to move about in.

A BV 202 over-snow vehicle which can wade but not swim. Note the passenger cab, which is articulated from the tractor.

There are times in a blizzard when no one can see very far. The horizon is lost, and the sky and land merge in a white flurry of snow known as a "white out." These conditions are dangerous for helicopters because the pilot cannot tell how far he is from the ground when he tries to land. Nor can he see overhead electric and telephone wires, which might bring down his chopper.

At such times, the landing craft can still feel their way up a fjord and are, therefore, invaluable in Norway, as they can bring supplies to troops who would otherwise be cut off from their parent ships or bases.

Some of the arctic kit worn or carried by a Royal Marine Commando

LCU with cover over tank well, known as the "Black Pig"

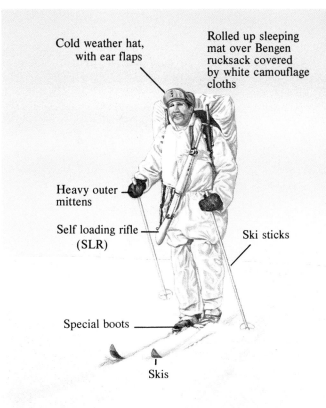

Cold weather hat, with ear flaps

Rolled up sleeping mat over Bengen rucksack covered by white camouflage cloths

Heavy outer mittens

Self loading rifle (SLR)

Ski sticks

Special boots

Skis

19 River Crossings

Many wide rivers like the Rhine in Germany, the Danube in Central Europe, and the Bug in Russia, can only be crossed by an amphibious force. The last such crossings to attack well-defended river banks were made in the Second World War, when, for example, British and American troops captured the northern bank of the Rhine near the German town of Wesel.

This battle began on Friday, March 23, 1945, after swimmers had made a recce of the German defenses on Thursday. The following afternoon, 40 storm boats were launched in a backwater on the south bank. At 5:30 PM, 150 medium bombers attacked Wesel, and at 6:00 PM, an Allied artillery bombardment began and continued until H-hour, 9:00 PM.

As the bombardment stopped, the first British marines landed on the north bank in 24 LVTs. Field guns then fired at the Germans, while the marines kept close behind this barrage, moving forward 330 feet (100m) every minute.

There were only 1,200 marine and army commandos, a small force to capture a sizeable town. Some followed the LVTs in the storm boats, which had outboard engines, while others were ferried across in the LVTs, which returned to the south bank after landing the first assault wave.

The commandos captured a bridgehead (as a river "beachhead" is called) on an uninviting stretch of mud, about $2\frac{1}{2}$ miles (4 km) west of the town. This was then bombed by 250 Lancasters, carrying twice their normal bomb loads. This air raid made the advance of the small force possible because the bombs flattened much of the town's defenses.

Nevertheless, the commandos had to fight their way across the rubble of bombed buildings.

On Saturday morning, around 10:00 AM, an American Airborne Division landed by parachutes and gliders north of the town. By early evening, they had linked up with the commandos. The next day, tanks of the British Twenty-first Army Group were ferried across the river to link up later with the American army which had crossed the Rhine over two weeks earlier, 84 miles (140 km) south-east of Wesel.

Future river crossings, which are usually strongly opposed, will be led by amphibious tanks, like the Soviet Russian PT-76 pictured here. Alternatively, crossings may be made by air-cushion (hover) craft, if they can be built with armor plate protection for the cargo-personnel.

A. In April 1945 commandos crossed the Reno River and the shallow Lake Comacchio, using storm boats as shown here to land onto a tongue of land between the lake and the sea. German defenses, heavily fortified strong points with mine fields and wire entanglements, were cleared on the first day. The next day, these men of 2 Commando Brigade advanced about 7 miles (12km).

B. In the 1980s tanks are built to wade rivers with little or no work required to make them waterproof. Some — like the Russian PT-76 pictured here — can also swim, either by the motion of their tracks or by retractable propellers or air jets.

C. In April 1945, 45 Commando's LVTs swam the Rhine when 1st Commando Brigade crossed this wide river to capture Wesel. They fought their way into the town and the next day joined 17 American Airborne Divisions that had landed parachute troops the previous night. This Commando Brigade — always known as "1st" not "l" Brigade — crossed four other rivers in 1945, all opposed crossings.

A

B

C

43

20 Combined Operations in the Future

Pictured here are several ideas of how a landing force might be brought to an enemy coast and then landed in the future.

The Landing Surface Effect Ship, an LSES, will use an air-cushion to lift its 13,000 tons for the last part of its voyage. It can then travel at 60 mph (100 km/h) over the water to launch an assault force. Each ship can carry nearly 1,000 marines, four large helicopters, eleven LVTP, and two LCAC. Or the load might be almost entirely helos in one LSES, with combat stores in another. Although it can be sailed as an ordinary ship with its hull in the water, it cannot be torpedoed in the usual way once it is lifted by the air-cushion. Also, it will be less likely to set off mines. But its greatest advantage will be its speed. The army defending the coast will have difficulty moving large numbers of troops to defend the landing place, which may be along 120-180 miles (200-300 km) of coastline, and which can be reached by the LSES in a couple of hours.

Another way to put men ashore may be in LVTs which crawl along the sea bed (see picture). These could be launched underwater by a large nuclear-powered submarine, and they would be difficult to hit with missiles during their run-in because they only surface in the shallows close to the defenders' bunkers.

Looking further into the future, marines may be carried in rocket-propelled space transports, which might be launched from a carrier as shown in the picture. Each spaceship, carrying 1,200 marines, would be fired to a height of 140 miles (235km) and return to earth 45 minutes later some 6,000 miles (10,000 km) from the launching site or ship. This is not as unlikely as it may seem. Already there are designs for 74 marines to be carried in an existing space shuttle.

However combined operations are carried out in the future, they will only be possible for nations with control of the sea. Therefore, nations must

A

have strong navies, air forces, and space forces if they want to land a force behind their enemy's main defenses, with all the advantages such landings have in shortening a war.

A. **A landing ship of the future with great fans lifting it on a cushion of air**

B. **A carrier of the future launching two rocket transports carrying marines**

C. **An impression of how a tracked amphibian might move along the sea floor**

Who will make certain that their landing point is free of the enemy? How will they be sent fresh supplies once they have been landed for some days? The tried and tested methods of past combined operations explained in this book will still be in use, for someone will have been sent there secretly to study the landing point. Some raiding force will secure the landing zone from enemy interference, and later there will be "Rocket Supply Ships" bringing in reserves of ammunition, food, and combat supplies. A war game, which has a serious purpose for Combined Operations in the 21st century, will involve using space just as we now use the oceans.

Glossary

Combined Operations Jargon

A1	First rate, good
Bandwagon	BV 202 oversnow vehicle
Belay last pipe	Cancel the last order
Bivvy	A bivouac or temporary shelter
Bootneck	One time the Navy's name for a Royal marine
Booty	Abbreviation of Bootneck; commonly used in 1980s
Buzz	A rumor
Chopper	Helicopter
Chuffed	Pleased
Clear Lower Deck	All personnel to attend a meeting
Common dog	Common sense
Crash-out	Go to sleep
Dig-out	Try hard
Endex	End of an exercise
Galley	Kitchen
Globe and Buster	Royal Marines cap badge of a Globe and Laural
Gonk	To sleep
Green maggot	Sleeping bag
Guz	Plymouth
Hand	An individual who is well thought of
Helo	Helicopter
Jack	A seaman in the Royal Navy
Lash Up	Make shift or give a party or presents
Leatherneck	At one time, any marine; in the 1980s, an American Marine
Make and Mend	Strictly a time for repairing your clothes but now used for time off work
Nutty	Sweets
Oolu/ulu	Jungle
Pit	Bunk or bed
Pompey	Portsmouth
Pongo	Royal Marine's term for a soldier
Recce	A reconnaissance trip, to observe details of military objective
Swan	An easy time

AE	Assault Engineer	combat stores	ammunition, rations, and other items like fuel and drinking water needed to fight a battle
AW	Amphibious Warfare		
AWT	Arctic Warfare Training		
BARV	Beach Armored Recovery Vehicle	Commando Unit	a force of between 450 and 650 men commanded by a lieutenant-colonel, equivalent to an army battalion
BMA	Beach Maintenance Area		
CAP	Combat Air Patrol		
Civgas	Commercial Gasoline	Commodore	the rank senior to captain in the Royal Navy
CLFFI	Commander Land Forces Falkland Islands	cargo-personnel	the men carried in a landing craft who are to be landed
D-Day	First day of an operation		
DP	Distribution Point	coxswain	the man in charge of a small landing craft like an LCU
DZ	Dropping Zone		
FOB	Forward Operating Base	davits	the curved metal poles that hold the smaller craft until it is lowered over the ship's side into the water
FOO	Forward Observation Officer or FO, Forward Observer		
GPMG	General Purpose Machine Gun	drowned vehicle	one that cannot use its engine because certain parts are too wet
H-hour	Time of Landing		
JS	Joint Services	flightdecks	the platform decks for helicopters or other aircraft
LCA	Landing Craft Assault		
LCOCU	LC Obstruction Clearance Unit	helos	helicopters
LCU	LC Utility	"hit" the beach	land on the beach
LCVP	LC Vehicle Personnel	inshore	close to the beach
LPD	Landing Platform Deck	logistics	the supply of combat stores to a force in battle
LPH	LP Helicopter		
LSL	Landing Ship Logistic	Ministry of Defense	British government department responsible for the fighting services
LST	Landing Ship Tank		
M&AW	Mountain and Arctic Warfare		
MGRM	Major General Royal Marines	offshore	out to sea, some way from the beach
ML	Mountain Leader		
POL	Gasoline and Lubricants	radio circuits	a series of radio links; although more usually in general conversation, the electric wiring of a radio
RM	Royal Marines		
RRC	Rigid Raiding Craft		
SAS	Special Air Service		
SBS	Special Boat Service	radio link	the contact by radio between two radio sets
SC	Swimmer Canoeist		
Tac HQ	Tactical Headquarters	Roll-on-Roll-off	describes the way vehicles may drive on and then drive off a ferry
USMC	United States Marine Corps		
air-cushion craft	use fans to lift craft by trapping air between skirts from hull of craft	ship's escorts	smaller ships which protect a bigger ship from enemy attacks
amphibious	involving both sea (navy) and land (army) forces	slipway	a slope built to haul craft up out of the water
Army Group	a force of several armies	stern gate	the stern (back) end of a ship that may be raised or lowered to allow vehicles to drive off the ship along a ramp
beachhead	the foothold an invading army establishes on the enemy's shore		
bed roll	marine's bedding rolled up so it may be easily carried	superstructure	those parts of a ship's upper decks, bridge, etc. built above its main hull
bongle	hand-operated mechanical instrument making percussive sounds which can be identified underwater and located by submarine.	tide line	the edge of the water which moves up a beach as the tide comes in
		water-gap	the water between the end of a craft's lowered ramp when it is beached and the dry land

Index